GONE
but NOT
LOST

Other Books Authored
or Coauthored by David Wiersbe

10 Power Principles for Christian Service

The Dynamics of Pastoral Care

Ministering to the Mourning

GONE *but* NOT LOST

GRIEVING *the* DEATH *of a* CHILD

REVISED AND UPDATED

DAVID W. WIERSBE

BakerBooks

a division of Baker Publishing Group
Grand Rapids, Michigan

© 1992, 2011 by David W. Wiersbe

Published by Baker Books
a division of Baker Publishing Group
P.O. Box 6287, Grand Rapids, MI 49516-6287
www.bakerbooks.com

Printed in the United States of America

Library of Congress Cataloging-in-Publication Data
Wiersbe, David.
    Gone but not lost : grieving the death of a child / David W. Wiersbe.—
Revised and Updated.
        p.   cm.
    ISBN 978-0-8010-1381-2 (pbk.)
    1. Children—Death—Religious aspects—Christianity. 2. Bereavement—
Religious aspects—Christianity. 3. Consolation. I. Title.
BV4907.W575 2011
248.8′6—dc22   2010042090

Scripture is taken from the Holy Bible, New International Version®, NIV®. Copyright © 1973, 1978, 1984 by Biblica, Inc.™ Used by permission of Zondervan. All rights reserved worldwide. www.zondervan.com

11   12   13   14   15   16   17   7   6   5   4   3   2   1

To
Mike and Pat Mulvain
and
Steve and Carolyn Scherrer,
who became my teachers as
they walked through the valley
of the shadow of death,
and whose lives today
continue to demonstrate that
God does give
beauty instead of ashes, and
the oil of gladness
instead of mourning.

Contents

Preface 9

1 The Wounded Parent 11

2 A Place Called Heaven: Questions Parents Ask 15

3 Out of the Depths 21

4 Part of You Is Gone 25

5 The Grieving Process 29

6 Stolen Identity 35

7 Grief Is Not Rational 39

8 The Tears of God 43

9 Styles of Grieving 47

10 Facts and Feelings 53

11 Ambushed 57

12 The Mourner's Creed 61

13 Marital Strain 65

14 Needing to Know 71

15 Guilt   75

16 Mad at God   79

17 Going Through   83

18 Questions   87

19 Danger: Platitudes   91

20 The Rope of Hope   97

21 Mary, the Mother of Jesus   103

22 Preserving the Memories   107

23 Resistance and Acceptance   111

24 Circle of Love, Circle of Grief   117

25 Special Situations   121

26 A Ready Response   125

27 A New Beginning   131

For Further Reading   135

Support Groups for Bereaved Parents   137

Preface

I AM GRATEFUL TO THE GOOD PEOPLE AT BAKER BOOKS for the opportunity to improve on the first edition of this book. Eighteen years is a long time for a book to survive, and I'm glad that *Gone but Not Lost* is getting new life.

Past readers have asked how I came to write this book. For several years, I attended meetings of The Compassionate Friends and Survivors of Suicide with my friends, Mike and Pat Mulvain. This was my apprenticeship in helping those who mourn. Eventually, the church I pastored began a bereaved parents' support group, and I became the facilitator. Each month I listened to the experiences of our group members. Over time common themes, complaints, insights, and questions emerged. Those whose grief was fresh complained about the lack of a concise written resource that focused on the basics. What I learned from my sisters and brothers in that group became the core of this book.

This book is intended for the newly bereaved parent. Use it as a compass on your journey through sorrow. Look at it as an emergency kit for those moments you encounter a crisis.

Grief interferes with our ability to concentrate, so the chapters are focused and brief. This is not an in-depth study on the stages and specifics of grief; rather, it is a starting-point and a locator as you move through your grief.

Death breaks relationships. Part of the pain of grief is having love to give but no loved one to receive it. The Christian's assurance and hope are that those who die in Christ are alive with him, and there is a day of glorious reunion coming.

A pastor said in a funeral message, "Our brother is gone from us, but he is not lost. When you know where someone is, he isn't lost. He is in heaven with Jesus. So he is gone from us, but he isn't lost!" This is the truth that sustains Christian people in their sorrow.

But—parents must still learn to live with grief and cope with marriage, family, work, and the rest of life. My hope is that this book will help you to understand what you are experiencing and provide encouragement and hope. Because of his death and resurrection, Jesus Christ is our greatest source of information and comfort.

I write as a believer in Jesus Christ and in the truth of God's Word; I write as a caregiver who wants to bring healing to the wounded; and I write as a pastor who has walked with members of his flock through the valley of the shadow of death. Jesus always welcomed children to be with him. I believe that when a young child dies, he or she enters the presence of the Lord.

May the God of all comfort be your strength in sorrow.

The Wounded Parent

In all their distress he too was distressed.
Isaiah 63:9

*B*EREAVED PARENT. THAT IS A DESIGNATION APPLIED TO you since your child died. You didn't choose it, and it is probably hard to accept that "bereaved parent" means you. Your child's death has changed your identity.

As a bereaved parent you have walked through these experiences:

- being with your child at the time of death, or being notified of your child's death;
- feeling numb and shedding tears;
- talking with medical personnel;
- making funeral arrangements (decisions you never expected to make);
- being surrounded by guests at the visitation, listening to so many words;
- sitting through the funeral, thinking "this isn't real";
- wondering when you'll wake up and this nightmare will be over;
- asking questions that have no answers;
- feeling a constant, inner pain;
- sensing that everyone's life is normal, except yours.

No one tells us how much death hurts. There is a physical pain to it, beyond description. Some parents have called it "the stomachache that never ends." There is a sense of dislocation—of being on the outside, watching events unfold. There is also the constant inner awareness that "This really is happening to me, right now."

It is not the normal course of things for a child to die before his or her parents. We expect our parents will die first, and then it will be our turn. No parent expects to make his or her child's funeral arrangements or witness the funeral.

Children die in so many ways: miscarriage, stillbirth, SIDS (Sudden Infant Death Syndrome), disease, accident, lingering illness, suicide, murder, or drug overdose. A child can die at any age. It is always tragic when a child dies. The death of a fifty-year-old son may hurt an eighty-year-old mother as deeply as a mother whose six year old dies.

Pain is a part of life, but the pain of grief is unique. It is hard to describe, harder to explain, and sometimes overwhelming. It takes strength to endure this pain, because no drug gives relief. The writer Samuel Johnson said, "Grief needs to be digested." It takes time to come to terms with the pain of grief.

In grief's agonies you are not alone. God cares about what you feel and what you are going through. God is not indifferent to your pain—he shares it. Consider this affirmation: "In all their distress he too was distressed, and the angel of his presence saved them" (Isa. 63:9).

When you hurt, God hurts with you and for you. It helps to go to someone who understands how you feel. When you go to God, he promises to comfort and give you strength. Truly he does care and understand like no one else. His Son died, too.

A Place Called Heaven

2

Questions Parents Ask

I will go to him, but he will not return to me.
2 Samuel 12:23

WHERE DO CHILDREN GO WHEN THEY DIE? THE Bible tells us they go to heaven, into the presence of God.

King David had an infant son who died when he was seven days old. David's response, "I will go to him, but he will not return to me" (2 Sam. 12:23), indicates that he believed his son was in a place that David would eventually reach. That place is heaven.

A child belongs in his or her parents' arms. That's how it should be. No other place could be better or safer for our child, or so we feel.

When a person dies, the soul leaves the body. Our bodies are "tents"—houses that the "real" us live in. St. Paul wrote that when we are absent from the body (dead), we are at home with the Lord (see 2 Cor. 5:8). He also seems to indicate that when a Christian dies, the Lord Jesus puts him or her to sleep, and they awake in heaven (see 1 Thess. 4:14). "Sleep" is one of the most common pictures for death in the New Testament. We don't fear sleep; it is something we need and desire.

The person who dies is not asleep. He or she is alive and fully conscious in the presence of God. Heaven is a place of perfection, so it is possible that children don't remain in childhood there. They may well grow up. In heaven, no desire goes unsatisfied, and all our desires there are good. There is no pain or grief in heaven. In heaven, earth's questions are answered. It is a place of joy, security, and love.

But we aren't in heaven yet. We hurt and we have questions. We also have a promise from Jesus: "Father, I want those you have given me to be with me where I am, and to see my glory" (John 17:24). Someday Jesus will gather all his followers to himself, and there will be a glorious reunion. This is what King David meant when he said of his infant son, "I will go to him."

Jesus is the way to heaven: "I am the way and the truth and the life" (John 14:6). Those who believe Jesus died for their sins on the cross and rose again to provide eternal life go to heaven when they die. Those too young to hear and understand the story of Jesus enter heaven, too, because God is just and gracious. He will not condemn a person who never had a chance to hear and believe. Jesus, who always welcomed children, has a place reserved for them in his presence.

Questions Parents Ask

1. *Our child was stillborn. Do we have a child in heaven?*

The Bible teaches that from the moment of conception, we are persons in the eyes of God (see Jer. 1:5; Ps. 139:13–16). Each developing, unborn child is a unique person. When the process of development ends with death, that child's soul enters paradise. It is good for parents to name a stillborn child and to have a funeral service. Yes, you have a child in heaven.

2. *My spouse and I come from different Christian traditions. We had our infant son baptized after he died, but it is still an issue. What should we do?*

First of all, it is important that parents feel they did everything possible for their child. If your faith tradition allowed for the child's baptism, and you followed it, be at peace. There are theological differences among Christians about infant baptism, but a child's funeral is not a time for theological debate.

Next, consider that salvation is God's gift to us through Jesus. God is loving and just, and will not keep a child out of heaven if the child was not baptized.

Finally, if you can agree that your child is with Jesus, then look forward to a day of reunion instead of reliving a disagreement about the past.

3. *Is my child an angel?*

Well-meaning persons may refer to a deceased child as an angel, but they are misinformed. Children are human beings, and a redeemed human being has a higher place in heaven than any angel. Angels are God's ministers who obey him and serve his people (see Heb. 1:14). God's people have a more intimate relationship with God than angels do. God the Son became human to save us. When we enter heaven, we become like Jesus: he "will transform our lowly bodies so that they will be like his glorious body" (Phil. 3:21).

4. *Will I know my child in heaven? Will he or she know me?*

Yes. The Scriptures indicate that people recognize each other in heaven. Because heaven is a place of perfection, those who died as infants or children may well have grown up. But you will know your child, and he or she will know you. "Now I know in part; then I shall know fully, even as I am fully known" (1 Cor. 13:12).

5. Does my child know how much I love and miss him/her?

I believe that God tells our loved ones in heaven as much as they need to know. Heaven's citizens are not primarily concerned with events on earth, yet what occurs on earth during our lifetime matters in heaven. Those in heaven understand the events of their earthly life and are at peace. If our loved one's joy in heaven requires some information about us, God surely communicates it. More importantly, *God* knows how much you love and miss your child who died, and he gives you his comfort and hope.

Out of the Depths 3

Out of the depths I cry to you, O LORD;
O LORD, hear my voice.

Psalm 130:1–2

I T FEELS LIKE DROWNING. YOU'RE IN OVER YOUR HEAD AND you can't catch your breath. When you do come up for air, you seem to get pulled back under. Each time you seem to go down deeper. It's the depths—the depths of grief and sorrow.

The depths are a confusing place to be. There seems to be no firm bottom. It's hard to tell what is real. You go through the motions of living but don't feel like you're alive. Life is out of sync; you feel dislocated. Sometimes in the depths you think about how much better it would be if life were over.

God is with you in the depths. The depths are what Jesus experienced as he died on the cross. The depths are not where you'd choose to be, but you are not there alone. Nothing can separate you from God and his love—not even death (see Rom. 8:38–39).

We learn some lessons in the depths that we cannot learn anywhere else. We learn to live by faith. A child's death makes us realize how little control we actually have in life. We can't trust ourselves, so we must trust God. It's the only way to survive.

We also learn to wait. Life can be lived only a breath at a time, an hour at a time, a day at a time. The depths slow us down and confront us with what matters most. As we wait, we get to know ourselves—and God. "Those who hope in the LORD will renew their strength" (Isa. 40:31).

Part of waiting is "waiting for"—we're waiting for something to happen. We're waiting for the pain to lessen, for things to make sense, for energy to keep going. Waiting is easier if we are "waiting with"—sharing the experience with someone else. We grieve alone, but we need others to share our grief. Who can wait with you? Whom can you wait with?

In the depths we learn to hope. Death will not be reversed. We know that. But hope is not "wishful thinking." It is a confident expectation for the future based on God's character and promises. God promises to see us *through* (see Isa. 43:2). He promises reunion with those who have entered heaven before us (see John 17:24). He promises to meet today's needs (see Phil. 4:19).

The question is "*How* will you go through the depths?" Put your trust in God—now.

Part of You Is Gone 4

Woe to me because of my injury!
My wound is incurable!
Yet I said to myself,
"This is my sickness, and I must endure it."

Jeremiah 10:19

WHEN YOUR CAR BREAKS DOWN, YOU GO TO A mechanic. He puts in new parts, makes adjustments, and your car runs fine again. When your body is ill, the doctor examines you and makes a diagnosis. Medication or surgery can cure the problem. With treatment, you're healthy again.

The mechanical and medical models do not help when it comes to grief. Part of you died when your child died. That part of you is irreplaceable. There are no interchangeable parts to get you through grief. You have to adjust. There is no simple process.

Think of your journey through grief as a kind of rehabilitation. When a woman loses her eyesight, there are ways of coping. She can learn to read braille, get a Seeing Eye dog, and learn to navigate with a cane. If a man loses his hearing, he can get hearing aids and learn to communicate through sign language and lip-reading.

Living through the aftershock of death can teach you new ways to adapt and survive. Life is never the same after a loved one dies. You will need to learn new ways of thinking, acting, and feeling.

Life is still worth living, but there are adjustments to make. They are not easy, because they require admitting that your child is no longer there. The adjustments can include not making as much food for a family meal; missing that precious face at the dinner table; not tucking your child into bed at night; buying fewer Christmas presents (or no birthday gifts); having tears come unbidden when surprised. You can make these adjustments as you walk through the grieving process. Determine that you will learn the skills needed to survive.

You will never forget your child. Your life will not be the same. As you go through the changes, you can hang onto God, because he never changes: "Jesus Christ is the same yesterday and today and forever" (Heb. 13:8). His love surrounds you. His strength is available to you, and he will help you face each demanding new day.

The Grieving Process 5

My soul refused to be comforted.
Psalm 77:2

Those who hope in the LORD
will renew their strength.
Isaiah 40:31

MOST AMERICAN BUSINESSES GIVE EMPLOYEES three days of funeral leave if the person who died was an immediate relative of the employee. On one hand, this policy recognizes a significant relational loss. On the other hand, it seems to imply that after three days off, the employee should be "over" his or her grief and able to function just like before. But grief doesn't work that way.

An acorn planted in fertile soil requires sun and rain—and many years—to become a tall oak tree. Growing from seed to mature tree takes T-I-M-E. Grief is a process, and that requires time. You will not "get over" your sorrow today or next month. In fact, no one can put a timeline on grief. It cannot be hurried along. Grief is also work, demanding concentration and choices.

Each person grieves differently. We walk through the stages of our sorrow in different orders. What follows is a brief summary of some of the experiences you can expect as you mourn the death of your child. You probably won't experience them in the order presented. Knowing what you are experiencing will affirm that you are normal—all grieving persons feel these emotions and think these thoughts.

Grief usually begins with *shock*, like being punched in the stomach so hard the wind is knocked out of you. Or it's like having a concussion, where it's hard to absorb information or think clearly. Shock is like nature's novocaine. There is a numbness and inability to feel as deeply as you think you should. Many times the funeral is over before the numbness wears off.

"I'll wake up soon and find out this is all a bad dream" is one way of expressing *denial*. It's hard to believe and accept that this is happening to you. Many grieving persons try to bargain with God at this point, saying, "I'll do anything to return my life to what it was like before." But nothing can bring your precious child back.

For some, *tears* come right away. Others take time to be able to cry. Grief must be expressed, and crying is one way for us to release our anguish. In our culture boys are taught that crying is a sign of weakness, and therefore men grow up unable to cry. But real men do cry, and tears are a sign of love and strength. The need to cry can last a long time.

"Someone's going to pay for this!" is a sign of *anger*. Anger is a hostile response to a real or perceived threat. We feel that someone or something is to blame. Some parents blame themselves, and some blame God. If your child's death was caused by a drunk driver or a sports injury, your anger has a specific target. Being angry is normal, but anger needs to be channeled in constructive—not destructive—ways. Angry outbursts may feel justified, but they provide only temporary relief. Getting stuck in our anger can damage us physically, spiritually, and relationally.

The feeling that you're drowning, overwhelmed by all the emotions and decisions and pain, can lead to *despair*. "I just don't feel as if I can keep going" is what grieving people say. That expresses how they feel, but they keep going in spite of the feelings.

Confusion feels like a tornado is snatching you up, spinning you around, destroying your connections to a normal life. Some mourners think about suicide. Others struggle with relationships. This is the point where grieving parents ask, "Am I going crazy?" The answer is no. This is how grief feels right now. Because you have probably never felt this way before, you don't recognize the confusion as part of your sorrow. It is unpleasant. It is also normal.

Every mourner tastes *depression*. It is bitter. Feeling like you're carrying a heavy burden, withdrawing from family and friends, and lacking energy for living are signs of being depressed. There is no way to experience the death of a child and not go through depression. Being with other people is good, though, and so is doing something for yourself. Seeing your doctor and using an antidepressant for a time may be necessary. Depression will come; you don't have to give it a permanent address.

When you begin to see a ray of light in your dungeon of darkness, it means you are starting to *hope*. Much of the grieving process looks back; hope dares to look ahead. The ability to laugh, see beauty in a sunrise, or enjoy a tasty meal means you are accepting that your life has not come to an end.

One afternoon Judy called her daughter's pediatrician. "Doctor Peterson, I'm calling to thank you for all you did for Nicole before she died. If you have time, I'd like to make an appointment for you to explain her disease to me again." For Judy, that conversation indicated she was coming to terms with her child's death. *Acceptance* comes only with time, but when you can say "I'm ready to hear the truth," acceptance has arrived.

When you find yourself ready for a new venture, it is the harbinger of a *new beginning*. The wounds may not all be healed, and the scars may be tender, but you're ready to begin a new chapter in life. You have suffered a severe loss. Going through grief has been a rehabilitation process for you in every area of your life. Attempting something new is a sign that you've learned the skills needed to move forward.

Not everyone goes through each of these "stages." You may cycle through some experiences several times. There is no "right" order. There is no magic time limit when you suddenly are done with grieving. Everyone grieves in their own way and at their own speed. You will know inside when the process is nearing completion. Grief is a process, and it takes *time* to digest. Give yourself permission to grieve.

Stolen Identity 6

By the grace of God I am what I am.
1 Corinthians 15:10

ONE CONSEQUENCE OF YOUR CHILD'S DEATH IS THAT your identity has changed, but you may not be aware of it for a while. It is not a choice you have made; rather, it was imposed on you from the outside. Your identity has been stolen.

You're still the person you were before your child died, but others see and identify you differently. Instead of being Mrs. Anderson or Elaine, you are now "the mother of that boy who died." It's not fair, but for a time, you'll be known by your loss.

Inside, you feel like you're the same person, except for the grief that has taken up residence in the core of your being. It's still you, but you're on an accelerated learning curve about death and pain and adapting. It's still your life, but you see it from a different perspective as the boundaries and rules of your existence are modified. You are who you were, only now you have an acute awareness of how deep life can go, and you're developing a new scale of priorities.

These internal changes show on the outside and people respond differently to you than before. A bereaved father told his group what happened at work when he returned following his son's funeral. "First my boss welcomed me back, told me how sorry he was, and told me to let him know if there was anything he could do for me. By the end of that week, he was upset because I clearly wasn't as productive as before. Within a few weeks my numbers were back up, but the boss called me in and told me I was 'damaged goods' and that I needed to look for another position."

Many bereaved parents have related a story similar to this one. Beverly was helping with a special event in her surviving son's class at school. Judy, another mother, was also helping. As they watched their boys play, Judy told Beverly, "I used to think you had the perfect life. Since your daughter died, though, every time I see you I see my worst nightmare." Beverly had to leave the room to cry and then pull herself together. She realized that people saw her through a different lens now—and she didn't like it.

What is most important is how you see and identify yourself. When grief is fresh, speaking of your loss is frequent and normal. As time goes by and healing progresses, you won't see yourself as a "bereaved parent" but as a person whose life experience now includes the death of a child and all that follows.

The death of your child hasn't changed your name or your character. It has broadened your experience of life and your awareness of what can go wrong. But, if you are grieving properly, it has also deepened your compassion, understanding, and concern for others. It has made you more grateful for your spouse, surviving children, and extended family—and for the small things that add richness to each day.

By the grace of God, you are who you are. You can't be who others expect you to be. You have to be yourself. Part of your identity is "traveler on the road of suffering." Your identity is what you decide.

Grief Is Not Rational 7

*Why is my pain unending and my
wound grievous and incurable?*

Jeremiah 15:18

PERHAPS THE MOST DIRECT WAY TO SAY IT," SHE SAID with a serious expression, "is that I think I'm going crazy. I feel out of touch. I feel like I'm losing it." The speaker was a mother whose teenager had died three months earlier. She looked healthy and dressed fashionably. She was handling things at work and holding her marriage and family together. To all appearances her transition through the grief process was going well.

But inwardly she was struggling. Sometimes this mom was angry; other times tears came unexpectedly and embarrassed her. She knew God loved her, but she also wrestled with how a loving God could allow her daughter to die just as her life was blossoming.

I knew a bereaved father who appeared to be the poster child for how to handle grief. However, this man spent hours thinking about his son's death and how he could have prevented it. He meticulously thought through the events of that day, agonizing over what he could have said or done to make the outcome different. At one point he said, "I feel if I can just get the circumstances in the right order, Todd will still be alive." If thinking could change history, this father would have worked the miracle.

Grief is not rational. The most rigorous logic in the world will not allow you to escape the ache inside. It is an emotional jumble. The feelings are real: emotional and physical pain; anger, depression, and confusion. The quest for understanding is also real, frustrated by the inability to find the key that could turn back time.

All these emotions and thoughts are normal during the grieving process. The fact that you feel and think these things says that you are *healthy*, even though you don't feel like it. You're experiencing what others have tasted in their walk through the valley of sorrow. You are not alone.

In some ways, those who sorrow are the healthiest people in town. They know they hurt. They express their feelings. They cry. They ask the tough questions they know can't be fully answered. They get mad and say angry words. For those in grief, this is normal. It shows their minds and hearts and bodies are functioning in healthy ways.

The Tears of God

Jesus wept.
John 11:35

*And God will wipe away every
tear from their eyes.*
Revelation 7:17

43

WHEN JESUS'S FRIEND LAZARUS DIED, JESUS WAS away. Jesus reached Lazarus's tomb four days later, and he stood there and wept. The Son of God shed tears over his friend taken by death.

What can we learn from the fact that Jesus cried?

Tears are natural. God made us with the ability to cry when we hurt. It's our body's way of releasing grief and tension. It is our heart's way of showing the depth of love and loss we feel. We'll cry many, many tears in our times of sorrow. God keeps track of every tear we shed (see Ps. 56:8).

Tears are a sign of love. Jesus loved Lazarus and was deeply moved when he died. I believe Jesus was angry at the pain death had inflicted on the people he loved (see John 11:33). You weep and sob because you love your child. You don't stop loving when someone dies.

Tears are a sign of strength. Our culture tells us that men shouldn't cry; we think it looks weak. Jesus was a strong man, physically and emotionally, yet Lazarus's death moved him to tears. The ability to cry says we can respond normally (with tears) to an abnormal situation (death). Persons who can cry are demonstrating emotional and spiritual health.

Grief is a time for tears and crying without feeling embarrassed or ashamed. The tears need to come—they're part of good grief. Those who know you and your situation will understand, and probably cry with you. Those who don't understand—their time will come.

One day the God who sees each tear that falls will wipe every tear away.

Styles of Grieving 9

I set my face like flint.
Isaiah 50:7

*Rachel [was] weeping for her children
and refusing to be comforted.*
Matthew 2:18

SOME PEOPLE CAN EXPRESS THEIR SORROW EASILY AND openly. Shedding tears is a necessary, healthy way to grieve. So are asking questions and feeling angry. Often sorrow removes our appetite and food loses its taste (though it is still important to eat). Some bereaved parents can reminisce about their daughter or son, and laugh or cry without hesitation. But others have a difficult time revealing their true feelings.

We're all alike, but we're also different from each other. For some personalities it is almost impossible to cry publicly or even discuss personal thoughts and feelings. These persons need to grieve privately, where few see their tears, hear their pain, or share their memories. What is most important is that each parent whose child has died be able to express his or her grief in some appropriate way.

When a wife can grieve openly but her husband is private about his grief, problems may arise. For instance, the wife may think her husband doesn't care about what happened, that he has no feelings. Of course that is not true. But the husband may also think his wife is overreacting, crying too much, and not dealing with reality. He may well be wrong.

Grieving is an individual process, and no two people go through it in the same way or at the same rate. A husband may express his grief through anger or withdrawal, while his wife may be starting to accept their loss. A wife may withdraw from her circle of friends and relationships, while her husband seeks people out. One spouse may quietly go through the family photo albums at home, while the other regularly mentions the deceased child in conversation with friends. Too much work can become an unhealthy escape from the situation. Tears can be a way to avoid responsibilities that should be resumed.

To navigate the rapids of sorrow successfully, spouses have to talk to each other about how they are experiencing grief. They share a common loss, but experience it individually. Expressing what each one feels and thinks will prevent husbands and wives from making faulty assumptions or reaching wrong conclusions. It will build bridges to each other's mind and heart.

Betty was an energetic and intense woman, and her grieving style was quite open. She cried when she needed to, talked about her emotions, and showed pictures of her daughter Shelly to those she spoke with. Dan, her husband, returned to his usual routine a week after their daughter's death. Betty never saw Dan cry, and when she talked about Shelly he would listen but then change the subject.

Because Dan's grieving style differed from hers, Betty came to believe that Dan didn't love Shelly and was just "cold." One day she came home early from work and found Dan in Shelly's room, looking at her baby book and sobbing. The walls Betty had built crumbled. She realized it was a mistake to assume that Dan would grieve exactly like her. From then on, Betty and Dan talked regularly about how they were adjusting.

Of course, some people would rather have a root canal than talk about how they feel. This is when a close friend or a pastor can assist a couple in being good communicators. Talking can bring the pain and frustration out of the dark and into the light, where healing can then begin. We cannot deal with what we will not name. Honest conversation can help us identify what bothers us and move us toward solutions.

It is a tremendous comfort to learn that someone else feels what you feel. It may not be felt in exactly the same way, but you are helped when you know you're not alone in your suffering.

Facts and Feelings

The LORD *gave and the* LORD *has taken away;*
may the name of the LORD *be praised.*

Job 1:21

If only my anguish could be weighed.

Job 6:2

THE FACTS ARE THERE ALL THE TIME, HAMMERING AT you. He died, a victim of disease. She died in the car accident. *My child is dead, gone. I am a mourner, a pilgrim on the path of sorrow.*

The feelings are there, too. Empty arms ache to hug and cuddle your child again. Eyes burn from too many tears. Stomachache, headache, heartache. Wishing it weren't true, wanting to be alone, wanting not to be alone. It's an emotional mess, and you're stuck in the middle.

At times, you may feel God hates you, or he is punishing you for something you did. You may feel as though God is far away and has forgotten you. You may be angry at God or even hate him. Those feelings, too, are part of grief.

Occasionally a peace may steal over you, but it doesn't last as long as you'd like. The emptiness commands attention, and your tears flow again.

We human beings feel many emotions, and many of them at the same time. Grief forces us to accept that we are human. Human beings suffer when someone they love deeply has died. We are complex creatures, and therefore cannot always understand what we are doing or feeling.

When the feelings are overwhelming, keep this fact in mind: Feelings are *real*, but feelings are not necessarily *reality*.

For instance, you may feel as if God is punishing you, but in fact God loves you. God loves you even though you feel he doesn't. Maybe you feel that life is no longer worth living.

The facts are that you still have much to live for, and there are people who need and love you. It is difficult to bring our feelings into line with what we know. Our feelings are real, but they need to be governed by the truth.

The man named Job experienced a series of disasters that wiped out everything he owned in a single day. The worst of Job's losses was the death of his seven children. He wept, was angry, and argued with his friends and God. But through his experience he never forgot the facts. He knew he'd been faithful to God, and he knew God would be faithful to him. He believed God was listening and that God cared for him. Job lived through the emotions of grief. But he based his decisions on the facts, not on how he felt. Feelings will change; God will not change, and his promises will not change.

Ambushed

They shoot from ambush at the innocent man;
they shoot at him suddenly.

Psalm 64:4

My heart is wounded within me.

Psalm 109:22

THE DAY IS GOING WELL. YOU'RE FEELING BALANCED inside, keeping up with your responsibilities and looking forward to a quiet evening. Then the radio station plays your late daughter's favorite dance tune. Your heart is wrenched and you begin to cry.

You finally decided to do some Christmas shopping. Knowing that you'll be buying fewer presents is depressing, but for the sake of your family you want to bring some joy to the season. After the first few purchases, you're feeling better. As you enter a store, a good friend meets you coming out, and she says, "Merry Christmas!" Like a cold slap in the face, you realize Christmas isn't going to be merry this year. The tears fall, your nose runs, you can't speak, and you head to your car without saying a word.

A graduation announcement comes in the mail, telling you that one of your son's friends is finally through college. You think, "My son would be graduating from college this spring, too. I wonder what he would look like. I wonder what challenges he would be ready for. If only. . . ." Other families are rejoicing; you're looking back and feeling the empty ache again. A nice day has turned gloomy.

Members of grief support groups call those kinds of experiences "ambushes." They're shots from the dark that you never see coming. When the ambush hits, the response is immediate and often negative.

There is no way to avoid ambushes. You can't possibly plan for every conceivable situation. They can happen at church, in the mall, in the car, or while mowing the lawn. Seeing a video clip, hearing the sound of his or her voice, or remembering a treat your child loved can open the waterworks.

Usually our outburst embarrasses us more than it does those we are with. The people who love us understand our responses and won't add to the pain of the moment. Strangers might wonder what happened, but they're strangers and don't need any explanation. Moments of recognition or panic may crush us with emotion, but it is only for a moment.

It helps if someone is with us when we are ambushed. Your spouse can change the topic of conversation, or suggest that it's time for your next appointment or errand. A friend can intercept a problem person before he or she gets to you. For a while you may need a "bodyguard," but eventually you must handle ambushes for yourself.

Ambushes are hard to deal with at first, but as we gain experience, we can handle the situation better. What used to make us go home and spend the rest of the day in bed now produces a few minutes of tears before we get back to work.

Ambushes are a reminder that we haven't completely healed yet. They're also good, because they tell us our hearts are still tender and we have not been hardened by our grief.

The Mourner's Creed

12

For when I am weak, then I am strong.
2 Corinthians 12:10

*I can do everything through him
who gives me strength.*
Philippians 4:13

WHEN WE GRIEVE, GOD SEEMS TO BE HIDING. It feels like he has abandoned us. He hasn't. In sorrow we feel as if nothing matters. It does. Sometimes we think life is no longer worth living; it is. In times of suffering, people of faith have to "believe against the grain." In our weakness, God reveals his strength, and enables us to go further or do more than we thought possible.

Faith means clinging to God in spite of circumstances. It means following him even when we can't see where he's leading us. It means being faithful to God even when we just don't feel like it.

Mourners need a creed: it is "I believe!" We need to affirm this creed daily:

I believe God's promises are true.

I believe heaven is real.

I believe I will see my child again.

I believe God will see me through this.

I believe nothing can separate me from God's love.

I believe God has work for me to do.

I believe God can turn loss into gain.

"Believing against the grain" means having a survivalist attitude. Bereaved parents are survivors—they have endured. Not only do they survive, but out of their grief they create something good. Your attitude toward your grief determines if the final result is health or sickness.

Before his son died of cancer, Pete was a hard, silent man. He didn't let anyone know what was going on inside him. He kept his thoughts and feelings to himself. In the months after his son's death, Pete was transformed. This "rock" cried in public. He talked about his feelings. He hugged his family members, much to their surprise. He made it a point to meet other bereaved parents and encourage them. In time Pete's life was marked by a transparent love and concern for others. He learned from his son's death how important people are and how important it is to *live*.

Grieving is hard work—but necessary work. Build on these foundation stones:

I will believe in God.
I will pray for God's help.
I will survive.
I will turn my grief to good, somehow.
I will enjoy life.
I will invest in the lives of others.

You may feel you're swimming upstream, believing against the grain. Attitude determines outcome—trust God and do the hard work of grief.

Marital Strain 13

Two are better than one. . . .
If one falls down,
his friend can help him up.
But pity the man who falls
and has no one to help him up!
Ecclesiastes 4:9–10

Love is patient, love is kind. . . . It always
protects, always trusts, always hopes,
always perseveres. Love never fails.
1 Corinthians 13:4, 7–8

THERE IS A DOMINO EFFECT IN FAMILIES WHEN A CHILD dies. It's as if crisis begets crisis. Husband and wife experience stress in their marriage. Parents and surviving children have conflict. The grandparents of the child who died may have issues with their children, the bereaved parents. Aunts, uncles, and cousins are affected. The natural order has been disrupted, and everyone feels it.

Think of your life as a huge ball of yarn with many strands of many different colors. Each colored strand represents one of the people you know and love. When one of them dies, the entire ball of yarn has to be unwound to remove the single strand. Then the ball has to be re-wound. That's a picture of what happens when a family member dies. Lives and relationships are pulled apart, and the results include tension and conflict.

Stress in a marriage and home after a child has died is normal. Each person grieves in his or her own way and progresses through grief at an individual pace. Family members are no longer in the same family: if the oldest child in a family of four died, each child has lost their oldest sibling, mom and dad are now parents of three children, and the grandparents have three grandchildren. If conflict is recognized and handled appropriately, healing will come. If not, more damage may be done.

Husbands and wives do struggle in the aftermath of the death and funeral. Many couples report problems with sex, emotional distance, and more arguments than before. Experts used to predict a high rate of divorce for couples after a child's death. Recent research has proved this prediction was wrong. But couples do have problems. If the child who died was the glue that held the marriage together, the couple must find a new foundation for their relationship.

Bad things don't have to happen. Here are some suggestions to help resolve the conflicts that can arise:

- Remember that each person grieves differently.
- Support your spouse physically, emotionally, and spiritually.
- Make time to express your thoughts and feelings about your child's death, your relationship, your needs, and your future.
- Give each other permission to grieve openly.
- Do things together, as a couple and as a family.
- Give your family permission to mark holidays and birthdays differently.
- Work together as a family to build unity and openness.

Some couples are afraid of sex after a child has died. It can be a lack of energy or an inability to focus on anything but the loss. Pregnancy may be a concern. There is also a danger in thinking that having another child can "replace" the one who died. Each child is unique, and therefore irreplaceable.

Husbands and wives need physical intimacy in grief. When both partners are willing, lovemaking can provide affirmation and comfort. For a start, at least talk about sex and where it fits into your marriage priorities now.

After God made Adam, he said, "It is not good for the man to be alone" (Gen. 2:18). Then God created Eve for Adam.

It is never good for humans to be alone, especially in time of sorrow. Grief shared can increase the bond between husband and wife and reduce the level of pain.

After their son died, Mark and Pam decided not to let their loss come between them. Instead, they would live in such a way that good results would come from this painful experience. They made investing in their marriage a priority. They continued going to church together and helped to start a support group. Their friends came to see Pam and Mark as a strong, loving team—because they faced their loss together.

Needing to Know 14

Now I know in part; then I shall know fully.
1 Corinthians 13:12

CURT NEEDED TO KNOW THE DETAILS OF THE AC-cident that ended his son's life. He interviewed witnesses, examined police reports, and quizzed the funeral director.

Susan questioned her daughter's doctors constantly, trying to understand the sudden death. She read dozens of books, and even called other families who had gone through a similar experience.

Some parents need to know as much about what happened as they can possibly learn. Knowing gives them a measure of peace. If that's you, that's okay. Direct as many questions as necessary to the right people. Most doctors, nurses, para-medics, police officers, and funeral directors are willing to answer your questions.

But other parents just don't want to know. Giving them more information than they want can be unfair and painful. Grief is easier for them by knowing less.

"Do you want to know about this?" is a good question to ask before seeking or revealing details about the death, funeral arrangements, or medical facts. If you are the person being told, retain your right to be treated with respect. If the conversation makes you uncomfortable, say, "I would rather not hear about this, please."

You have the right to decide whether or not to know the details. Others should respect your decision. Neither choice is wrong; make the one right for you.

15 Guilt

But with you there is forgiveness.
Psalm 130:4

I F ONLY I HAD CALLED THE DOCTOR SOONER." "WHAT IF we'd stayed home that morning?" "Did we try every possible treatment to save her?" "Did he look both ways before crossing the road?" "I should have known something was wrong!" "I wish I had expressed myself with different words."

Those comments—and many more like them—go through the minds and come from the lips of bereaved parents. A weight presses on your mind and heart, becoming a personal burden of guilt about your child's death.

When something goes wrong, people assume there has to be someone to blame. Many parents realize their child's death was no one's fault, but they feel guilty and blame themselves. Guilt, someone said, is anger turned in on ourselves.

It is normal to feel some guilt when a child dies. Parents are supposed to protect their children. It is hard to believe that a parent couldn't prevent a child's death. But insisting on being responsible for a situation you cannot change is unhealthy. Blaming yourself will not bring healing, only deeper wounds. Self-inflicted punishment is not good grief.

Maybe you had an argument with your son before he died, or you said something to your daughter you want to take back. Some parents have accidentally caused their child's death. Guilt for those kinds of experiences may be right. There is relief from such guilt: confess what you said or did to God. He will forgive you. Your child in heaven already understands and forgives. No one holds a grudge in heaven. God forgives. Your standards cannot be higher than God's: forgive yourself.

False guilt is destructive. You may need to talk with a counselor about the situation to get a more balanced point of view. No one can heal up while constantly re-opening the wound.

Mad at God 16

*But Jonah was greatly
displeased and became angry.*

Jonah 4:1

"EVEN IF GOD DIDN'T CAUSE MY CHILD'S DEATH, HE certainly allowed it!" stated an angry parent during a support group meeting. Many heads nodded in agreement.

Anger can be aimed in many directions. Some grievers take it out on their spouse or boss. Others vent their wrath on the doctors and nurses, the pastor, or the funeral director. The child who died can be a target for anger, too.

When we're angry, God is a convenient and safe target. He doesn't hit back. Lots of people have been angry with God, and God has always been big enough to take it.

Anger is hostility aroused by a sense of being wronged (whether the wrong is real or perceived). A child's death is wrong—and it provokes anger.

Anger is an honest emotion that needs proper expression. Suppressed anger can turn into headaches, ulcers, or a heart attack. But it's hard to admit being angry at *God*. After all, God is in charge. We fear that his response to our anger will be to judge us, or just ignore us. Our fears are unfounded.

Anger is like fire: if it is properly harnessed, it can do much good, like a furnace that heats your house. But left to burn uncontained, anger's fire will certainly cause damage. Decide that when your grief produces anger, you will use the anger constructively.

Admit that you are angry. Acknowledging the feeling is real gives you the opportunity to examine why you're angry.

Trying to hide anger never works; anger eventually rises to the surface. Holding it in only guarantees an explosion later on.

Perhaps you are angry about what your child's death denies you—all the good experiences of helping a little one grow to maturity. You feel cheated. Maybe your child was killed by a drunk driver. Maybe not knowing what really happened is what makes you angry.

Once the source of anger is identified, there are actions you can take to channel anger's power. You can work against alcoholism. You can raise funds to help with medical research. One mother, whose anger came from not knowing why her son died, became a hospital chaplain so she could comfort those who walked the same path. Another grieving mom decided to bake bread for someone each time the anger threatened to take over.

If it's a person you're angry at, you may need to talk with him or her—not to inflict pain, but to understand what happened and possibly to forgive. Forgiveness can extinguish anger's fire. It is not easy to forgive, but God can help you do it. If there are legal factors in the situation, it may be wise to get legal advice before contacting the person.

Please don't try to hide your anger from yourself or God. Face it honestly, and it won't control your life.

Going Through 17

When you pass through the waters,
I will be with you;
and when you pass through the rivers,
they will not sweep over you.
When you walk through the fire,
you will not be burned;
the flames will not set you ablaze.

Isaiah 43:2

THE KEY WORD IN THIS SCRIPTURE VERSE IS *THROUGH*. God promises you will get *through* the waters of grief, the river of sorrow, and the furnace of pain. God will see you *through*. What you experience today will not last forever.

One encouragement in this passage is that God knows who you are. He is your Creator, and he calls you by name (see Isa. 43:1). You are his, and God always takes care of his own. When we grieve, we feel unimportant and insignificant. But God knows you, and you are important to him.

God also knows where you are. He knows when you're fighting against the current of sorrow's river, and he knows when you're in the fiery furnace of suffering. Others may not know what you're experiencing. On the outside, everyone may believe that you're fine, but inside you are drowning. God knows, and he is there with you.

When Daniel's three friends were thrown into a furnace, the king watched (see Dan. 3:22–26). What he saw amazed him: the men were not harmed, and a fourth person had joined them in the furnace. It was Jesus!

God knows how you feel: alone, afraid, uncertain about the future, worthless. God made you, with all your emotions, and he knows how they can make you doubt and control you. God will never condemn you for the way you feel. Tell him how you feel—he will listen and understand.

God knows what you need when you grieve. You need someone to share the pain and to walk through the long valley with you. He promises his presence. He also promises his love: "You are precious and honored in my sight, and . . . I love you" (Isa. 43:4). God gave you his Son to conquer death and provide hope.

We have to live on promises, not on explanations. Even if God explained in detail why your child died, the answer wouldn't end your heartbreak or stop your questions. Instead of explaining, God gives us promises that keep us moving toward healing and hope.

You will get through your grief. The journey will be long, but there is an end. Live today and let tomorrow take care of itself. Use today's energy on today's challenges. God will provide fresh strength for tomorrow.

You're going to make it through.

18 Questions

My God, my God, why?
Mark 15:34

Teacher, don't you care if we drown?
Mark 4:38

GRIEVING PERSONS ASK QUESTIONS, LOTS OF QUESTIONS. We need information to make sense of what we're experiencing, and the quickest way to get information is to raise a question. If you have a question, ask. Don't worry about what people will think. You want to know, and the question burns within, so *ask*.

Some questions asked by bereaved parents have no answers. At least, there is no one on earth who can provide a satisfactory solution. Many of your weightiest questions involve God. For people with a deep faith, the questions can be difficult to ask—but ask.

- How can a loving God allow something horrible like this?
- I've been faithful to God. Where is God now that I need him?
- Why *my* son or daughter?
- Why did this happen?
- Why did this happen now?
- How can this be God's will?
- I hurt so badly; doesn't God care about me?
- Am I being punished for a previous sin?
- I'm really angry at God; will he hate me now?
- How strong does God think I am?
- When is this going to end?
- Will I ever be normal again?

Many hurting people asked similar questions in Scripture. They did not always receive answers. Job threw all sorts of questions at God; in the end, what he got was a longer list of questions from God (see Job 38–39)! Even Jesus, on the cross, asked God, "Why?"

Some say that questioning God is a sign of doubt. Actually, asking God questions is a sign of faith. Because we believe God is there, because we believe he has reasons, we query him. If we didn't believe in God, we wouldn't waste our time with such questions.

Receiving detailed answers to our questions would not relieve the pain of our grief. Even with a full explanation, life would still require major adjustments. Rarely does God explain himself. But he does give us his promises.

Some of your friends may try to answer your questions. Beware of people who have all the answers! Wise friends and caregivers know that mourners ask questions as a way to express what they feel. They don't expect a full response—and wise friends listen and don't try to explain.

When you ask the tough questions, that is evidence you take God and your faith seriously. God knows you need to make sense of your life. He hears your questions; he sees your tears. Promises are his response.

Danger: Platitudes

19

I have heard many things like these;
miserable comforters are you all!

Job 16:2

A PLATITUDE IS A REMARK THAT IS OVERUSED AND therefore meaningless and annoying. A grieving family who must greet the public at a funeral visitation hears too many of these commonplaces of grief. When a well-meaning but thoughtless person spouts platitudes, the best response may be to listen and say nothing.

"*God won't give you more than you can handle*" sounds biblical and is widely quoted. But it is not true. The platitude is based on 1 Corinthians 10:13: "No temptation has seized you except what is common to man. And God is faithful; he will not let you be tempted beyond what you can bear. But when you are tempted, he will also provide a way out so that you can stand up under it."

St. Paul is dealing with *temptation* here, not the overwhelming circumstances of grief. His argument is that God will help his children to escape the pressure to do wrong. That is the meaning of the verse, and the correct application. Those who extrapolate "God won't give you more than you can handle" and apply it to the crushing burden of grief are over-reaching.

Has God ever given anyone more than they could handle? I believe so. Do we really want to know the limits of our endurance? Probably not.

What about the man named Job? In one day all his flocks and herds, his sources of wealth and position in the community, and all seven of his children were taken from him. Then Satan attacked Job's body with painful boils. Job sat on an ash heap in torn clothing, scraping his sores with a broken piece of pottery. His wife said it would be better if he would curse God and die (see Job 1–2). I believe Job got more than he could handle.

And yet, Job kept going. He survived. God gave him the grace to do it. It was more than Job could handle alone, but not more than Job and God could handle together.

"*You have to accept God's will*" is another annoying bit of advice. On one level, of course we must accept God's will; there is no way to change things. At another level, we do have to come to terms with what God willed, and we have to wrestle with why he willed it. But anyone who believes that God takes joy in the death of a child is morbid and unbalanced. A possible reply is, "God doesn't owe me any explanations, and only he knows what's in my heart."

"*God took her to spare you something worse*" is sure to raise your blood pressure if not your temper. What could be worse than having your infant die in your arms, or reading in a telegram that your child was killed in battle? This kind of platitude is dangerous because it presumes to know more about God and your child than anyone could know. A nod, a "thank you," or a quick smile is a sufficient response.

Those who speak in platitudes want to help you feel better. They don't intend to increase your frustration. They probably have not thought through how their words might come across; they are using familiar phrases to attempt to connect with you.

This should make us think about *how our words affect others.*

Living "in the depths" of grief imparts a wisdom that cannot be expressed in trite ways. You are experiencing the words of Isaiah that also reflect the Lord Jesus: "The Sovereign LORD has given me an instructed tongue, to know the word that sustains the weary," (Isa. 50:4). Platitudes blow in the wind. Truly comforting words, mined in the tunnels of grief, are worth their weight in gold.

The Rope of Hope 20

*Not one word has failed of all
the good promises he gave.*

1 Kings 8:56

JUST AS A MOUNTAIN CLIMBER RELIES ON A ROPE FOR SUPport and protection, those who mourn rely on God's promises. God's words, spoken to us in time of need, enable us to "hang on." Here is a brief collection of promises for those who mourn. These are God's promises for you to claim whenever you need them.

> In all their distress he too was distressed,
> and the angel of his presence saved them.
> In his love and mercy he redeemed them;
> he lifted them up and carried them
> all the days of old (Isa. 63:9).

> The LORD is my shepherd (Ps. 23:1).

For God so loved the world that he gave his one and only Son, that whoever believes in him shall not perish but have eternal life (John 3:16).

I am the resurrection and the life. He who believes in me will live, even though he dies; and whoever lives and believes in me will never die (John 11:25–26).

God will wipe away every tear from their eyes (Rev. 7:17).

> He who goes out weeping,
> carrying seed to sow,
> will return with songs of joy,
> carrying sheaves with him (Ps. 126:6).

Blessed are those who mourn, for they will be comforted (Matt. 5:4).

Come to me, all you who are weary and burdened, and I will give you rest (Matt. 11:28).

Praise be to the God and Father of our Lord Jesus Christ, the Father of compassion and the God of all comfort, who comforts us in all our troubles (2 Cor. 1:3–4).

> When you pass through the waters,
> I will be with you;
> and when you pass through the rivers,
> they will not sweep over you.
> When you walk through the fire,
> you will not be burned;
> the flames will not set you ablaze (Isa. 43:2).

For I am convinced that neither death nor life, neither angels nor demons, neither the present nor the future, nor any powers, neither height nor depth, nor anything else in all creation, will be able to separate us from the love of God that is in Christ Jesus our Lord (Rom. 8:38–39).

My grace is sufficient for you, for my power is made perfect in weakness (2 Cor. 12:9).

My God will meet all your needs according to his glorious riches in Christ Jesus (Phil. 4:19).

Here are some Scripture verses to use as a response to God's promises:

> When I am afraid,
> I will trust in you.
> In God, whose word I praise,
> in God I trust; I will not be afraid (Ps. 56:3–4).

> His compassions never fail.
> They are new every morning;
> great is your faithfulness.

I say to myself, "The Lord is my portion;
therefore I will wait for him" (Lam. 3:22–24).

Cast all your anxiety on him because he cares for you (1 Pet. 5:7).

Be joyful in hope, patient in affliction, faithful in prayer (Rom. 12:12).

Mary, the Mother of Jesus

21

Near the cross of Jesus stood his mother.

John 19:25

H E WAS BORN IN DIFFICULT CIRCUMSTANCES, BUT she loved him. His stepfather died while he was a boy, and being a single parent took its toll on her. But she raised a fine boy to be a man.

When he went out on his own, she worried. But everyone seemed to like him, and he was popular. She relaxed. Then people began talking against him—important people.

He was accused of crimes he did not commit and statements he did not make. In a mockery of justice, they sentenced him to death. She saw him shamefully executed. The child she carried all those months, the little boy who played around the house, the man who carried on the family carpentry business—she saw him die.

The *pieta* (a statue of Mary holding the crucified Jesus) reminds us of the agony of the mother of Jesus. "Is any suffering like my suffering?" (Lam. 1:12). Grieving parents identify with her.

Mary's tears fell at the foot of the cross. Her heart was broken and her dreams shattered. "A sword will pierce your own soul," Simeon had prophesied (Luke 2:35). She knew the heartrending pain. And yet—she believed in God. What God had promised about her son's birth came true; God would still be faithful to the rest of his promises.

And he was! God raised Jesus from the dead. His resurrection is our source of strength and hope. Because Jesus died and rose again, death is not the end. There is the promise of reunion in his presence one day. And Jesus returned to life, affirming that life is worth living.

You may be thinking, "But Mary got her son back!" Yes, she did—for forty days. After Christ's ascension into heaven, Mary had to live by faith like every other Christian. She is a model for our own discipleship. We won't get our children back in this lifetime. Like Mary, we have to live by faith.

22
Preserving the Memories

Can a mother forget the baby at her breast?
Isaiah 49:15

YOUR CHILD'S DEATH DOES NOT ERASE THE FACT THAT he or she lived. It is a natural instinct to want to preserve the memories you and your family have of your child. But it should be done in healthy ways that allow you and your family to grow and change while remembering.

Mary and Paul wanted a memorial for their daughter that would bring joy and beauty to other people, the way Julie had done. They finally decided to plant a special tree in a park near their home. They worked with the local park district to make the arrangements. The dedication service was beautiful, attended by family and many of Julie's friends. A friend read a poem written for the occasion, Mary said a few words, and another friend offered a prayer. A plaque was installed near the tree, explaining the tree's special purpose and keeping Julie's memory alive.

Some families establish a memorial fund in the name of the child who died. The monies are then used for charitable purposes, and the family knows that good is being done in their child's name. The pediatric unit of a hospital, or a local EMT unit, is an appropriate recipient of such funds.

Tommy loved attending Sunday school. He looked forward to being with his teacher and friends each week. After he died, Tommy's parents made a donation to their church to refurnish the area where Tommy's class met. A plaque with Tommy's photo was hung in his classroom to preserve his memory and to indicate that his influence lived on.

It is good to remember your child's birthday. You may not want to celebrate, but reminiscing about his or her birth, and other birthdays, will help bring healing. Tears and laughter will probably mingle; that's how life is. Visiting the cemetery helps some families, as long as they remember the child is not there but in heaven. Telling stories about the child who is gone, but not lost, is important at family gatherings. It affirms this person was part of your lives and recognizes his or her influence on each of you.

Photographs provide an excellent record of your child and family. A family portrait on the living room wall keeps the memory alive. Some families make a special scrapbook or slideshow, and view it often. Seeing the pictures, and your child's drawings and letters, will remind you of much that was good.

The anniversary of your child's death is not a happy one. Some families try to ignore it. Others have a memorial prayer service or do something special for other people in the child's name. It is better to plan for the day, even if you do nothing special, than to let it sneak up and ambush you.

Choose ways of remembering that are comfortable for you. Think back over happy times you enjoyed together and your child's personal triumphs and joyous moments. Your memories will bring laughter, sorrow, and gratitude. Do not worry, you will never forget the child you love. By keeping his or her memory alive, you ease your own grief, and your family's.

23
Resistance
and Acceptance

*How often I have longed to gather your
children together . . . but you were not willing!*
Luke 13:34

A WOUNDED PERSON INSTINCTIVELY WITHDRAWS from others. Solitude seems preferable to society. There are no looks to avoid, no words to speak, no questions to answer, no tears to have to hide. "Please leave me alone," is a statement many grieving persons make.

Although you feel like being alone, what you truly need is to be with other people. You're not your normal self, and grief doesn't allow you to be who you want to be. But talking and crying with family and friends is good therapy.

Grief resides deep within us, and for healing to occur the grief has to come out. One of the best ways to bring grief out is by being with others who have walked the same path you're on now.

There are many support groups for grieving parents (a short list is provided in the appendix). Churches and hospitals sponsor groups, some that meet year-round and some that are for only a few weeks. A quick search on the internet (bereaved parent support groups) should give you a number of options close to home.

Each person who attends a bereaved parents' group knows what it is to have a child die. Meetings are led by sensitive survivors who can guide a helpful discussion on loss, grief, and healing. Parents at every stage of the grieving process attend the meetings and find help.

A support group is safe. You don't have to talk if you don't want to. Tears are common; they don't make anyone uncomfortable. Feelings are expressed and accepted. No judgments are passed. Questions are raised; no one has all the answers.

Most meetings begin with introductions. The person or couple facilitating the meeting might begin by saying, "We're Don and Marty, and our daughter Michelle died from cancer when she was fourteen." Not everyone can say this out loud. But the value is in being able to tell what happened, and hearing it from your own lips helps you to face reality.

Often there is a theme for the meeting, and there may be a guest presenter to talk about the theme. As the discussion deepens, people tell their stories and what they have learned— what helps and what doesn't.

It is good to discover that your thoughts and feelings are not yours alone. A support group provides reassurance: what you are going through is normal for a grieving parent. That lesson cannot be learned in isolation.

Parents who have been in the group longer are a source of wisdom. They know how to respond to situations you're facing. They know the right words to say. They give genuine encouragement because they have survived.

While a support group can be a lifeline, prepare yourself before you attend your first meeting. When grief is fresh, it can be difficult to hear others discussing their feelings with blunt honesty. It is wise to grieve for several months and then try out a group. Usually, attendees are sensitive to the needs of the newly bereaved and they ease you into the experience.

Some groups have a "bring a friend night" where the program is designed for first-time attendees. If you're resisting the idea of attending a group, ask a friend or your pastor to go with you.

When grief is fresh, your instincts will resist invitations to talk about your experience. If you accept that you need time with fellow-travelers on your path, a support group can become a place for healing, friendship, and guidance.

Circle of Love, Circle of Grief

Mourn with those who mourn.

Romans 12:15

GRIEVING PERSONS TEND TO FOCUS ON *THEIR* FEEL-ings, *their* needs, *their* day. This is normal; they don't have much energy to invest in others.

But when a child dies, the entire circle of family and friends is affected. Not only are there bereaved parents, there are bereaved grandparents, bereaved siblings, and bereaved friends. It's easy to forget how large the circle of grief is. It is good to discover you are not alone in your sorrow.

Each person touched by the child's death will grieve differently. For grandparents, the death of a child can be violently unnatural. It may increase their sense of mortality. They grieve not only for their dead grandchild but also for their adult child whose son or daughter has died.

Bereaved siblings, especially those still living at home, urgently need their parents and will continue to make the usual demands. Parents will have less energy to meet those demands, but honest and healthy grieving can help a family cope. For the entire family, it is important to keep living rather than withdrawing from life. Children should continue in Scouts and sports and school activities. If your family attends church together, keep it up. If you regularly went out for dinner on Friday night, stick to the routine. It provides a sense of normalcy in an abnormal situation.

Children grieve differently than adults. Parents should give children as much information as they can handle. Be honest about your feelings and tears, but let children know they should express their own feelings and ideas in their own way. In some ways children are more resilient than grownups, and can re-enter life more readily. Of course, they don't understand the full significance of their loss, so as they grow up, conversations about their deceased sibling will be repeated at deeper levels.

When your family gathers, talk about your feelings. Reminisce about the child who died. Laugh and cry together. This will allow everyone to grieve in healthy ways and keep the bonds of love strong. If a family member needs time alone, give him or her space and privacy. But make sure that person remains a part of the group.

Surviving children need to ask their questions, and in time they will have questions they may not quite know how to ask. For instance, if it was their oldest brother who died and he was a good student and athlete, younger brothers may wonder if they're expected to be like him. Children need permission to be who they are and do what they're good at, and should be liberated from false expectations.

Every family member's position changes when a child dies. The number of children, siblings, and grandchildren is reduced. Everyone is reorienting themselves to the new reality and new family dynamics. This, too, is a process. Being aware that the entire family is unwinding the ball of yarn and then re-winding it will assure you that things are normal, for a grieving family.

Special Situations

Is any suffering like my suffering?
Lamentations 1:12

SOME CIRCUMSTANCES CAN INTENSIFY AND COMPLICATE a bereaved parent's grief, and some situations are almost too painful for words.

What about when a parent experiences the death of a child not once, but two or three times? A genetic illness can lurk in a family's genes and turn fatal when a child is four or ten years old. Some couples have experienced multiple miscarriages or stillbirths. Grieving does not get easier with experience.

Car accidents and house fires can cause multiple deaths. Our hearts break for the father whose wife and four children were killed in an auto accident, leaving him to face the future with one surviving child. Each child has to be grieved individually, so the time of grief is lengthened. The loss upon loss makes for a crushing burden.

At this writing, America is still at war in Afghanistan and Iraq. Almost every day the military reports that men and women in uniform have been killed in action. There is the agony of knowing your child died far away, in an act of violence. Then there is the wait while his or her body is brought home. A military funeral pays solemn honor to the fallen, but the playing of "Taps" haunts those who mourn.

The women and men who serve our communities in the police force, as firefighters, or as paramedics put their lives on the line, too, and sometimes they die in the line of duty. Because of the more public nature of these deaths, their families have the added duties of responding to the media and trying to guard their privacy.

Many families who had a loved one die in the terrorist attacks of 9/11 had their grief complicated by the absence of a body. Being able to see and touch the body confirms that the person has died, gives opportunity to express love and say goodbye, and enables the family to carry out the public rites of grief (visitation, funeral service, and burial). A memorial service is the appropriate response when there is no body, but a sense of finality and closure is elusive.

When a child dies and his or her parents are separated or divorced, the emotional tension between parents can become more of a focus than dealing with grief in healthy ways. A divorced, single parent may feel more isolated than a partner who remarried. The remarried partner has to grieve with a spouse who is not the deceased child's biological parent. If the couple have children who live with each parent in turn, these siblings need to be able to grieve their loss without having to choose "sides" between mom and dad.

A child's death and funeral will expose any relational issues in a family. The mature decision would be to put relational differences aside, encourage the entire family to grieve in healthy ways, and postpone personal agendas until the funeral is over. Avoiding the "blame game" is crucial, as is any expression of "I loved her more/she loved me more."

Properly handling the above situations may require the services of a grief counselor. Your pastor or funeral director can certainly help you start identifying the issues. A family that has gone through a similar situation can also provide wise counsel.

A Ready Response 26

*A word aptly spoken
is like apples of gold in settings of silver.*

Proverbs 25:11

ONE OF THE SENSITIVE SITUATIONS YOU WILL FACE is responding to persons who raise the fact of your child's death. Most people who do this do not intend to add to your pain, but questions and comments will come and you need to be ready with a response that allows you to control the conversation. Good responses indicate that you have suffered a loss and the topic is open for discussion—but you have set limits on the extent of the conversation.

"Do you have children?" is a common conversation starter. For a bereaved parent, it can also start tears flowing. Whether your loss was a stillborn son or a forty-year-old daughter, a good response is "We have ___ children here, and one in heaven."

"Do you have only one child?" is more difficult to answer. Why do other people make your family life their business? One mother at a support group meeting told her story: "A nosy woman kept asking why, at my age, we hadn't provided a sibling for our daughter. At first I felt embarrassed; then I started getting angry. Finally, I said that she had a brother, but he died of SIDS at six months. The woman realized what she had done, turned red, apologized, and walked out of the store!" Next time, the questioner was probably much more sensitive.

In an attempt to find an explanation for why your child died, people may say without thinking, "God must have had a reason for this." A reason—beyond your understanding—might exist, but their statement sheds no light on your experience, and it affords less comfort than the speaker intends. One wise father responded to such well-intentioned but misguided statements this way: "Yes, I'm sure God has his reasons. But he hasn't told me what they are, and I sure miss my boy a lot."

More sensitive persons may preface a question or comment with, "I don't want to hurt your feelings." Some folks think it an act of kindness to avoid mentioning your child or the death. Saying, "It hurts more to not talk about my daughter" communicates that you're ready to talk about her.

"Aren't you over it yet?" usually comes from people who are threatened by the reality of death. It is an insensitive, judgmental question that implies there is something wrong with you. Your response should be free of any guilty feelings. "No, I'm not over it yet, and I probably never will be. My heart is broken, and there are scars I will carry all my life. I am getting better, though—and part of a healthy recovery is talking about my child."

"If only you'd had more faith" can cut painfully deep. This comment should tell you that the speaker's own faith in God is threatened by your experience. When these words come from a church friend, or a pastor, it can be devastating. But there are several ways to respond without getting into a long theological debate. "I believe God did his will and I accept it" affirms your faith in God and your maturity in facing reality. "A lack of faith didn't take my son's life. It was the lack of self-control in an alcoholic driver," points out that life is woven from complex factors. "I don't use my faith to manipulate God. I will trust him no matter what problems I face" may be the best response of all.

"But—you have other children!" moves our thinking from the individual to the group. But our children don't come in groups; they are individuals. While the remaining children are a source of comfort, strength, and joy, they can never replace the child who died. Each child is a unique gift from God, leaving a special imprint on our hearts and lives. "Yes, I'm glad for each of my children; but Matthew was Matthew, and I'll always love and miss him" makes the point.

Some of the comments you hear will hurt. They will reveal how little others know of your experience. Try to be patient. Your friends love you and don't always have the words to say what they feel. "A word aptly spoken" can silence busybodies, correct wrong assumptions, and open the door to meaningful discussion.

Sometimes friends don't visit as often as they once did. They haven't forgotten you. As one man put it, "I don't know what to say to Jim and Ann, so rather than say the wrong thing, I say nothing." Reminding friends that you like to have your child remembered can set them at ease. Real friends won't stay away long.

There are people who cannot cope with the reality of death, so they avoid you. One couple reported to their support group, "We were in the grocery store, and at the end of the aisle we saw two of our friends. They saw us, looked at each other, and went down a different aisle!" Try not to be offended by their immaturity. Your strength may challenge them to change.

A New Beginning

27

I am making everything new!
Revelation 21:5

His compassions never fail.
They are new every morning;
great is your faithfulness.
Lamentations 3:22–23

YOU PROBABLY DON'T FEEL LIKE IT NOW, BUT SOMEDAY you'll be ready to start living again. That day cannot be rushed, but it will come.

When your child died, so did a part of you. Your world stopped. You did the things that had to be done. You went through the appropriate social motions. Then all the activity stopped. You cared for the follow-up decisions with insurance companies, hospitals, and the funeral home.

Your friends and relatives went home after the funeral and seem to have gotten back to normal. But there is no "normal" for you. It's a struggle to get up and get through the day. Dealing with people exhausts you. But you're doing it, with help.

God's response to death is always life. That doesn't mean he gives another child when one dies. It means that out of the sorrow and ruin of your "other" life, God gives you a new life. It grows on you slowly, as you work through your grief. God gives you "beauty instead of ashes, the oil of gladness instead of mourning" (Isa. 61:3).

One indicator of making a new beginning is the ability to laugh. Often laughter is thought inappropriate—even a sin—in time of sorrow. Memories will prompt smiles. It's okay—and good—to be able to laugh about what was funny. It's also important to be able to laugh at yourself.

Another sign of a new beginning is not worrying about what to say in response to people's questions. After Don died, Kaye was uncertain what to say when new people asked how many children she had. She decided to say, "I have four kids at home, and one son in heaven." That told people she had experienced a death in the family, but affirmed her willingness to talk about it.

A sure sign of a new beginning is your desire and ability to help others who are grieving. Having experienced God's comfort, you want to share it. "Praise be to . . . the God of all comfort, who comforts us in all our troubles, so that we can comfort those in any trouble with the comfort we ourselves have received from God" (2 Cor. 1:3–4). When you are full enough inside to be ready to give, the healing is almost complete.

Some years after his daughter's death, Tom was let go from his job. His severance package included tuition costs for retraining. Tom returned to school to learn how to be a grief counselor. His goal was to take what he'd learned from Tarah's death and use it to help other bereaved parents. This proved to be the right decision for him. It was Tom's new beginning.

For Further Reading

Alcorn, Randy. *Heaven*. Wheaton, IL: Tyndale, 2004.

Bayly, Joseph. *The Last Thing We Talk About: Help and Hope for Those Who Grieve*. Colorado Springs: David C. Cook, 1991.

Burton, Jehu Thomas. *Trusting God Through Tears*. Grand Rapids: Baker Books, 2000.

McKracken, Anne, and Mary Eemel. *A Broken Heart Still Beats: After Your Child Dies*. Center City, MN: Hazelden, 1998.

Schiff, Harriet Sarnoff. *The Bereaved Parent*. New York: Crown Publishing, 1987.

Westberg, Granger E. *Good Grief*. Philadelphia: Fortress Press, 1971.

Wolterstorff, Nicholas. *Lament for a Son*. Grand Rapids: Eerdmans, 1987.

Support Groups for Bereaved Parents

The Compassionate Friends
www.compassionatefriends.org
877-969-0010
P.O. Box 3696
Oak Brook, IL 60522
The mission of The Compassionate Friends is to assist families toward the positive resolution of grief following the death of a child of any age and to provide information to help others be supportive.

First Candle (formerly SIDS Alliance)
www.firstcandle.org
800-221-7437
1314 Bedford Avenue
Suite 210
Baltimore, MD 21208

GriefShare
www.griefshare.org
800-395-5755
P.O. Box 1739
Wake Forest, NC 27588

GriefShare provides grief recovery support groups for a wide range of grief experiences. There is a thirteen-week cycle of topics, and you can enter at any point.

MADD—Mothers Against Drunk Driving
www.madd.org
800-438-6233
MADD National Office
511 E. John Carpenter Freeway
Suite 700
Irving, TX 75062

SHARE (Pregnancy and Infant Loss Support)
www.nationalshare.org
800-821-6819
The National Share Office
402 Jackson Street
St. Charles, MO 63301

Each of the above groups offers a "group finder" on its website. Additionally, newspapers in urban areas often provide a weekly listing of support groups.

David W. Wiersbe has served four congregations in the Evangelical Free Church of America and is currently serving at Calvary EFC in Spring Grove, Minnesota. He was a chaplain for a Fire/Rescue unit for twelve years, and is an experienced grief support group leader. David is in his fourth decade of pastoral ministry. He is coauthor with his father, Warren W. Wiersbe, of *10 Power Principles of Christian Service*.

The Empty Chair

HANDLING GRIEF *on* HOLIDAYS
and SPECIAL OCCCASIONS

SUSAN J. ZONNEBELT-SMEENGE, R.N., ED.D.

and ROBERT C. DE VRIES, D.MIN., PH.D.

"Help and hope for all who face the holidays anxiously
because a special loved one is absent."

—JAMES R. KOK,

director, International Conference on Care and Kindness,
Crystal Cathedral

There is hope for a brighter tomorrow.

Written after the death of the author's own child, *Surviving the Loss of a Child* offers you compassionate encouragement born from deep sorrow. You will find no pat answers or patronizing panaceas here— just real words of healing from someone who has been exactly where you are now.

Discover how you can go on living and reclaim hope in your heart.

Revell
a division of Baker Publishing Group
www.RevellBooks.com

Available wherever books are sold.

TRUE STORIES OF HOPE AND PEACE AT THE END OF LIFE'S JOURNEY

R Revell
a division of Baker Publishing Group
www.RevellBooks.com

Available wherever books are sold.